# PORTFOLIO

## GERALDINE'S COLLECTION OF CAKE IDEAS

MW01706534

Published 1994 by LESOME PRESS
3 Tannery Court, Richmond Hill, Ontario Canada L4C 7V5.

COPYRIGHT 1994

ISBN 0-9692523-3-1

All rights reserved. No part of this publication may be reproduced, stored in a retrieval system, or transmitted in any form or by any means, electronic, mechanical, photocopying, recording, or otherwise, without the prior written permission of the author.

Design and Production by RAFFI NERSESIAN & ASSOC./Raffi Nersesian

Photographed by GADI HOZ PHOTOGRAPHICS/Gadi Hoz, Amir Gavriely and LESLIE STUDIOS/Gordon Leslie

Printed and Bound by METROPOLE LITHO, Toronto.

Precious Moments ornaments supplied by customers for their cakes, frames 21 and 60, Copyright Samuel J. Butcher Co.

Cake decorating supplies by CREATIVE CUTTERS
561 Edward Ave. Units 1 & 2, Richmond Hill, Ontario
Canada L4C 9W6.

# ACKNOWLEDGEMENTS

I would like to thank Diane Temple for her wonderful gumpaste flowers, Joyce Norris for cutting my stencils, Raffi Nersesisan for co-ordinating the production of this book under stressful deadlines, Helen Low for her beautiful work on frames 61, 63, and 64, Carole Faxon for the airbrushed cakes shown on frames 47, 48, and 50, and finally a special thanks to both Nicole and Alan Randlesome for their dedicated support.

# FOREWORD

I am greatly honoured to forward Geraldine Randlesome's fourth book, Portfolio. Geraldine's innovative style and creativity has made her work instantly recognizable the world over. She is acknowledged as an expert in theory, who has perfected many styles of cake decorating including such techniques as the floating collar and no-bridge string work. Geraldine is in demand as a world class teacher, having taught in North America, South America, Europe, Australia, and Africa. She openly shares her techniques and ideas with others, motivating many of her students to win top awards for their work.

Unlike her previous books, which initiated the concept of line drawings and pictures followed by detailed instructions, Portfolio is another first, in terms of an ideas book solely of colour photographs of cakes designed for her clients. These splendid pictures, with their diversity ranging from elegant wedding centre-pieces to commercial and holiday cakes, are designed to stimulate and encourage both the novice and the professional cake artist. Due to its versatility as a catalogue of ideas, Portfolio is sure to expand one's decorating horizons.

*Carole Faxon*

Carole Faxon
U.S.A. 1994

# INTRODUCTION

Having been in the cake decorating arena for many years, I have gratifyingly witnessed the growth of sugarcraft enthusiasts around the world, as well as an equal, and impressive growth in the quantity of instructional materials for the craft. I now feel that the time is right for something a little more than just another cake decorating book to be available.

Portfolio, my latest contribution to the field, is the first full coloured photo album of cake designs - a sourcebook, to generate new ideas. Once the basics of decorating have been mastered, the next real challenge is one of creativity. This book is intended to help break that barrier and to stimulate the imagination. As such, Portfolio is a supplement to the standard instructional books that are currently on the market.

The photographs presented here are a cross-section of cakes made at my retail shop, "Creative Cutters". Portfolio is evidence that in a busy bakery, where cake decorating time is a restricted luxury, elaborate and artistically pleasing cakes can be produced despite stressful time restraints. Portfolio was planned with both professionals and casual cake decorators in mind. This book should be of help, no matter what level of skill you have reached. Included are a variety of styles and presentations to appeal to different tastes. Since wedding cakes are an important part of a decorator's repertoire, a special emphasis was placed on that category. In general, many of the designs can be easily adapted by removing certain symbolic items and by substituting them with other motifs to suit the occasion. Use Portfolio as a resource book of possibilities!

I hope that Portfolio will become a useful edition that you will turn to again and again for inspiration.

Geraldine Randlesome

Geraldine Randlesome
Toronto, Canada 1994.

# CONTENTS

***1. WEDDING BOOK***

**2. ROSES AND BOWS**

**3. SIMPLY YOURS**

**4. ROSES AND RUFFLES**

5. RIBBON FOLLIES

6. POLKA DOT

*7. PETALS AND IVY*

8. GOLDEN WEDDING

9. HEATHER

10. RUFFLED DOILIES

***11. VICTORIAN LACE***

12. BEGINNINGS

**13. FORGET-ME-NOT**

14. PRETTY IN PINK

15. BRIDAL GAZEBO

16. TOUCH OF PEARLS

17. GARDENIA TEMPTATION

*18. SWEET PEAS AND RUFFLES*

19. DREAMS COME TRUE

20. BUTTERFLIES

***21. WEDDING PARTY***

***22. CALLA LILY COMPLIMENT***

23. ROMANCE

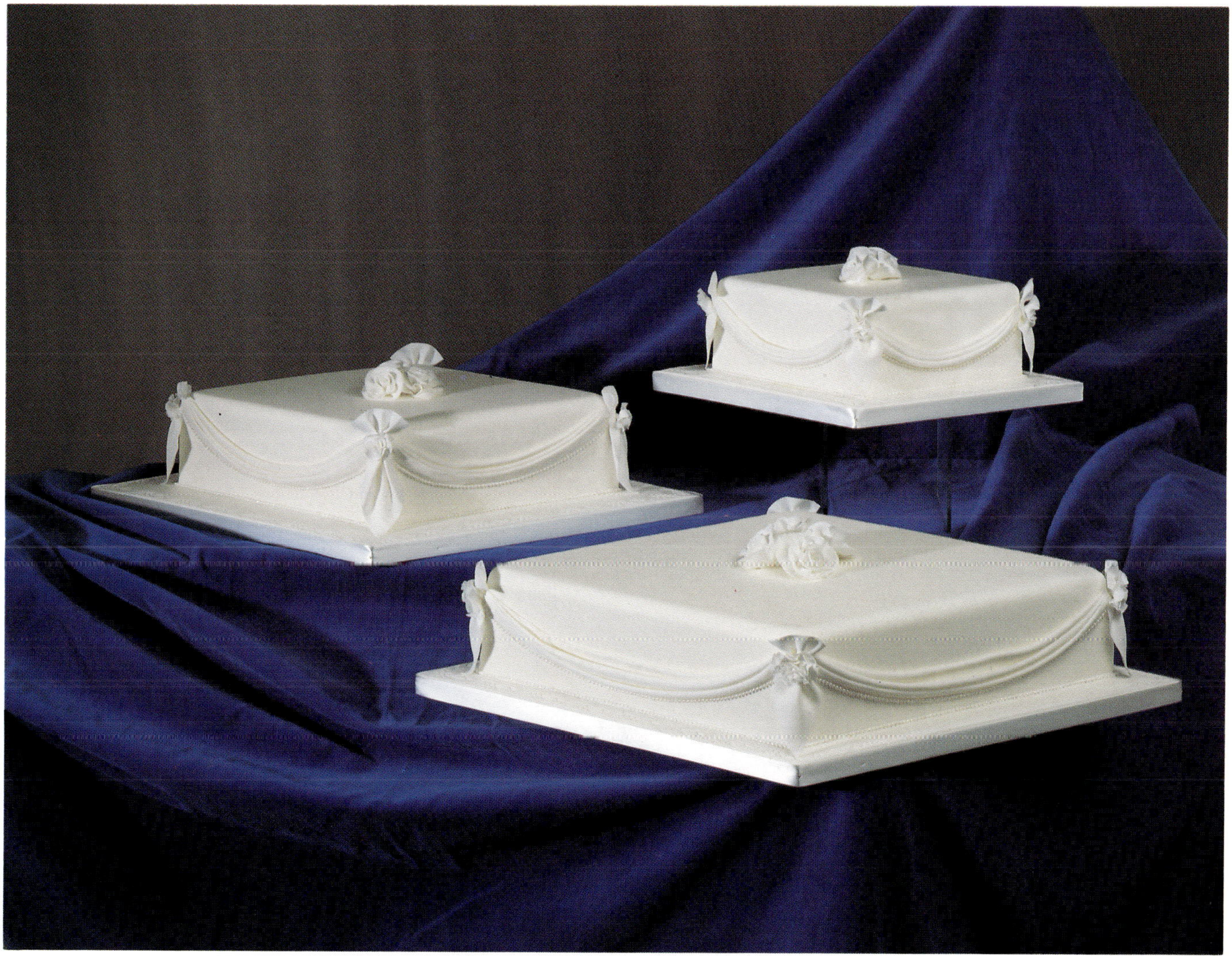

24. ELEGANCE

25. TRUE LOVE

**26. SWEET FORTUNE**

27. VICTORIAN CHARM

**28. FOREVER HEARTS**

29. BRIDAL FEATHERS

**30. GARDEN OF DOVES**

**31. CUPIDS AND THISTLES**

32. DREAMING OF CUPIDS

*33. SPRING-TIME FANTASY*

**34. VICTORIAN ROSE**

**35. SUMMER BLOOMS**

36. CASCADING ROSES

37. RADIANCE

38. BLACK LACE SOPHISTICATION

**39. IN LOVE**

**40. FLORAL COURTYARD**

41. CANOPY OF JOY

42. CANOPY OF JOY (DETAIL)

43. PIRATES

**44. TEDDY BEAR LOVE**

**45. BIRTHDAY WISHES**

**46. WELCOME BABY**

***47. MY DAY***

***48. PRETTY AS A PICTURE***

**49. ANNIVERSARY**

50. ELEGANT LADY

**51. TEDDY BEAR'S FIRST BIRTHDAY**

52. HOLLY BERRY HAPPINESS

53. FAMILY CHRISTMAS

54. HOLIDAY HOLLY

55. CANDY CHALETS

56. CANDY CHALETS

**57. CHRISTMAS PETITS FOURS**

58. ROSE TRELLIS

**59. GOLDEN YEARS**

60. BALLERINA RUFFLE

61. EASTER EGG HUNT

*62. BOW TIE STRINGS AND FUCHSIAS*

63. TEA PARTY

64. TEA PARTY (DETAIL)

THE PHANTOM OF THE OPERA
PANTAGES THEATRE
MON NOV 20 1989 8:00 PM

***65. SHOWTIME***